# About the author

William Middleton is a Combat Army Veteran having done three tours in Iraq. He is a father and a husband.

Don't Play with the Madness

# William Middleton

## Don't Play with the Madness

Vanguard Press

VANGUARD PAPERBACK

© Copyright 2024
**William Middleton**

The right of William Middleton to be identified as author of
this work has been asserted by him in accordance with the
Copyright, Designs and Patents Act 1988.

**All Rights Reserved**

No reproduction, copy or transmission of this publication
may be made without written permission.
No paragraph of this publication may be reproduced,
copied or transmitted save with the written permission of the publisher, or in
accordance with the provisions
of the Copyright Act 1956 (as amended).

Any person who commits any unauthorised act in relation to this publication
may be liable to criminal prosecution and civil claims for damages.

A CIP catalogue record for this title is available from the British Library.

ISBN 978-1-83794-527-6

This is a work of fiction. Names, characters, businesses, places, events and
incidents are either the products of the author's imagination or used in a
fictitious manner. Any resemblance to actual persons, living or dead, or actual
events is purely coincidental.

*Vanguard Press is an imprint of
Pegasus Elliot Mackenzie Publishers Ltd.*
www.pegasuspublishers.com

First Published in 2024

**Vanguard Press
Sheraton House  Castle Park
Cambridge  England**

Printed & Bound in Great Britain

# Dedication

For my grandmother, Mary; my wife, Melissa; all my close friends, and my two boys who encouraged me to push myself.

# Acknowledgments

I would like to thank Audrey Harpp, Kimberly Moore, Ann Berenger, Amber Putnam, Bridget Putnam, Anna Silburn, Cassy Sehlmeyer, Linda Sehlmeyer, and Sarah Belanger.

# Don't play with the Madness

"This house is for you and the kids"
Don't look through those curtains
Look at this for face value
Don't see that meaning
Please don't read deeper
Don't look at that part
Please don't remember the past
Your statement stirred fear
Shit, she almost cried
Don't cry for me
Don't hate my statement
Don't reach for my heart
It's my soul that needs saving
The mind is too far gone
But can the soul be saved?
But the madness?
You can't unbake a cake
Be careful in there
Don't play with the madness
It's fragile

# Take Me Now

Nearly every moment
Emotional and physical pain
Torture every step
The torture of every thought
Painful revelations
It's almost easier to dangle
Better to leak it all
Sweeter to fire
The torture of every thought
Killing me slowly
Wasting me away
Eating at the happiness
Feeding on joy
What do I do?
Where do I go?
Just please
Take me now!

# Frozen Moments

Since moment one
The little hand wrapping my finger
Warmth flushing my being
My job has now started
Always with your safety in mind
Little milestones remembered
Little moments frozen in time
It is now my job
Make sure you never suffer
Guiding you along the path
Fight by your side
Ensure you both are a gentleman
Instil respect in others
Push you to succeed
Both are brilliant
Show you that you can be anything
Teach you the ways of the world
Each little moment that passed
Now frozen in time
Moments frozen in my heart
I'm proud of you both

# Private Wars

Deep alone in the darkness
The madness thrives
You have but one step ahead
Ignite the fires of truth
As madness fights and fades
Stuck in the confines
A heavily guarded nightmare
Needles bouncing on the record
As the music of life skips
Repeatedly bombarded
By self-depreciating lies
Blinded from any form of truth
Self-worth and confidence
As real as a purple sky
Loathing the reflected self
Afraid of passing intentions
Slowly welcoming the dark
When does MY war end?
Cause I'm running low on ammo!

# Queen of the Temple

The first time I saw you
Was the first time I loved you
Seeing through
Seeing the real you
Falling for you that first moment
Falling deeper every other time
Every day I see you
Loving you more
I knew that first day
I had to make you mine
Had to convince you to stay
Loving you with words
Loving you with action
Showing you every day
Proving my love to you
Enter my temple
Be careful of my heart
It's barely holding on
You are here with me now
Make yourself at home
As the queen
The queen of my temple

# Twinkle

Standing here staring
Staring at the lights
Like thousands of flashlights
Hanging in the blackness
Past loved ones searching
With spotlights to find their family
Looking for who needs help to cross
Dancing in the night sky
Flickering and bright
Which one of them is you?
Which one do I need to look for
To talk to
Ask advice
Now that you're not here
You must be there
You must be one of those lights
Dancing in the darkness
Together with dad
There with grandpa
Just gotta find you
Gotta keep looking
Keep twinkling grandma
One day I will be there with you
Dancing and twinkling myself
Deep in the dark

# Fake It

Keep quiet
Don't tell
Don't let on about the pain
Just smile
Keep going
Every moment in a grin
No one cares about the pain
Grin, and bear your Demons
Hold them close
Don't let them see the scars
Keep your open wounds secret
Move through life
Quiet and smiling
They don't care if you hurt
Just keep faking it
Until you finally make it

# Scars

Little and large
There to remind you of the pain
The torment
And torture
Physical and mental
Cast deep on your soul
Cast across your psyche
Always remembering
Twisting your senses
Twisting your thoughts
Scars others can see
Others, you only feel
Hiding in plain sight
Do you hide them from others?
Do you fight your fight alone?
Hiding who you have become
The monster you are now
Snarling deep in your soul
The monster they created
The monster you desperately try to control
Medicated, you wander life
Praying for an end
Someone take down the monster within
Tired and alone, you fight

Creating more scars
Licking the open wounds
When do we heal?

# In My Rain

Safe haven and cozy
You bring light to my darkness
Within my disparity, you shine bright
Always on my mind
You have shown me true love
Best of friends
Deeper than just lovers
I long to wrap my arms around you
Save you from your darkness
You have shown me freedom
The true meaning of love
Together we fight Demons
Both yours and mine
Lean on me, for I am your pillar when in need
As you are mine
Drunk on lust every moment we are together
I hunger for your love
I need your presence
I miss your scent
Come to me and I will save you
As you have saved me time and time again
You are the sunshine
When I am in my rain
Find me in the dark
Shine your light bright

# Wash Me Away

Flooded tears
Rolling away
Washing away the pain
Flooding the anguish
When does it end?
Where did it begin?
Unexpectedly and sudden
The loss is dreadful
Flood my being
Pour out my heart
Lay it out for all to see
Naked and vulnerable
Shedding this being
Exposing new soft tissues
Making myself anew
Scrub down the sins
And wash them away
Take my hand
Walk me through this dark
And wash me away for good

# Set Me Free

Lower and lower I go
Deep in this hole
Creaking and groaning of the ropes
All because of the rope
The sweet release of pain
Letting it all go
Loved ones will hate
Loved ones will be sad
Left behind and tormented
Feeling their torment
As I am lowered in
Second guessing this moment
Wanting to go back
But all I wanted
Was, to be set free
Set me free of the pain

# In This Hole

Deep and dark
Drowning in tears
Suffering in the self-oppression
Beaten by self-doubt
Wanting so desperately to be normal
Trying to climb out
But I don't even have a ladder
No footing to find
Self-expiration looks better each day
Shivering in the dark
All loved ones peering in
Trying to lend a hand
I just can't reach
What is wrong with me?
Why do I hurt myself so?
Why do I torture my soul?
Why must I stay,
Deep in this hole of despair?

# Please Don't go

Every moment spent without you
Is a moment of loneliness
Every time you leave
My smile leaves with you
Every time you're with me
Butterflies are in my stomach
Every moment spent with you
Is a magic I can't explain
I love you with everything I am
So moments without you, are painful
Fireworks and fires of passion
When we are together again
I beg and plead
For one more second
For any more moments together
Please don't go
Please don't take my happiness with you
Don't leave me lonely
Don't leave me saddened
Don't let me contemplate an end to all of this
Worrying about you gone for good
Stay with me, please
Just please don't go

# Let Go

Holding on tightly
So tight it hurts
Hold every moment
As if it's the last
Slowly you realize
You hold the wrong thing
You value the wrong thing
You only realize now
After your already broken
Pieces of the puzzle
Strewn across time
Thrown across spaces unknown
Sometimes you must let go
If you value it most
You have to let it run
Let them lose
If it's meant to be
It will come back
Just let go

# Lost to Me

So many to care for
So little care for one's self
Little to no love
For myself
Hatred and disappointment
For me
I am lost in the dark
Alone and afraid
Demons haunt me
So many say to reach out
Look for them in the dark
But where are you?
You're not here
Few have ventured
Into the dark with me
Few say they love
Yet don't show that love
Can't be reached in the dark
Their hand is not found here
Lost to me is the love
The love you say you have
Where are you all?
I can't find you here
So it may be time to say goodbye

I can't keep looking for you
I have other hands to hold
To guide me out
Out of the abyss
Out of my head
You have been lost to me
Where did you go?

# Lost and Found

We knew each other once before
Years pass
You were lost to me
I have searched
You slipped past me
But now I have found you
Years have past
Only a few things changed
But not your beauty
That has retained
I have you back
More important to me than ever
As we slowly reconnect
A passion burns within
Passion for one another
The undeniable urge for one another
So here we are
Together at last
You were once lost
And I'm happy you are now found

## Mean Green

\*Puff\* puff \*
Cough
As I look at the twinkle
I'm sorry gram
I have to for relief
For quiet in my head
\*puff \* puff\*
Cough
Where is my quiet
It's just puffs away
Breath deep
Hold it in
Together we float
The still waters run deep
Slowly your mind sleeps
Shutting the voices down
Silence slowly creeps in
Finally relief
It's quiet here
It's unfortunate though
Gram wouldn't be happy
Not about this
I look at the twinkle
I'm sorry it took this

Just for relief
All because of
The mean green

# Break the Madness

Random thoughts in my head
Scary imaginings run rampant
Find the cord it says
Any braid will do
Make sure it will hold you
Don't fuck up this time
Where's the glint?
Any old sharp will do
Make sure it's sharp though
Can't fuck this one up
Find the gun
We don't own that though
You did this on purpose
We have to put a stop to this
These random thoughts
This is madness
It hurts to think about it
Why must we remember
Something must be done
To break the madness

# When it's Time

Here I sit waiting
Anxious and desperate
For an end to the pain
Is being loved enough
To deter my Demons
Why do they haunt me so?
One day they will leave me alone
I hope
But slowly the hope fades
Leaving room only for doubt
Leaving room for hate
Room for self-loathing
One day they will come for me
White sheet covered
Pine box clad
And when it's time
I will go for that final ride

# Beautifully Broken

Sitting there with so much on your mind
Silent, yet beautiful
Broken moments in time
Worry you so
As I sit here and admire your beauty
My love for you is eternal
I reach out to catch your pieces
To help put you back together
You may resist the help
But I'm still here
Lost in your own dark room
But I'm here to be your light
Here to be your rock
You're here for me
Now it's my turn
I sit and admire
How you're beautifully broken to me

# This Moment

Hold on
Slow down
Make the moment last
Let's take our time
Don't leave me yet
Studying your face
Every inch
In case I don't see you again
My heart swells
Only in your presence
Almost to bursting
Without you, I can't breathe
Without you, I can't speak
When you're not with me
I am useless
I am not whole
When I'm not with you
I long for your warmth
I long to hear your voice
That sweet angel bell in your throat
When I'm with you I hold on
I hold on to the moment
Every moment I can

In the case, I never see you again

# You There!

You there, in the gown
Long, and flowing, and beautiful
When did you grow so?
Almost an instant trip
Once a little girl stumbling to keep up
Yet now, graceful you glide
Grown to a woman so quick
He looks upon you still, proud
Silent whispers
Guiding your goals
Frozen moments in time we all share
An ironclad family surrounding you
You there, ironclad and strong
Strong and courageous
Facing life, head-on
Talent like no other on the field
We are all proud to know you
Proud of this graceful lady
Tracing out your own life
Carving your own place
Give the world hell
Show them you can be more
More than the stumbling little girl

# When's a Good Time?

Everything aches
The pain is unbelievable
Mental pain is unbearable
The haunting images
Hateful thoughts
Murderous images
Itching to get out
The self-hate boils
Never trusting yourself
Don't trust your thoughts
I'm now on borrowed time
Life is coming up short
When will it end?
Is it time to turn in the cards?
When is it my time?
Is that time soon?
When is a good time?
To cash in my chips

# I'm Sorry

I'm sorry
You had to go so soon
You had to bury your children
That I wasn't there when it was time to go
We didn't visit more often
I'm sorry
You were tormented so
By a man who hated life
All those years ago
I tried my best
To be a good grandson
To love you with everything I had
I'm sorry
It wasn't good enough
Because you still had to go
I'm sorry
I didn't try harder
I couldn't save you
I couldn't help you
I'm sorry
I'm here and you're not
I'm sorry
I'm devastated
I'm sorry

I cry myself to sleep
Most of all
I'm sorry
I can't join you

# It's Not Over

That voice
It tells you to go
It tells you it's over
You don't deserve life
Fills you with hatred
Hating yourself
It's full of shit
Push past it all
Look for your silver lining
It's there
You just haven't been seeing it
This is life
This is beautiful
Beautiful people care
You have tried before
You have failed
It was for a reason
You might have setbacks
Everyone does
But the fight isn't over
Life isn't done
It's not over
You're still here
You're loved

# Unlike Minded Warriors

Hidden away in the dark
You're kept away from the outside world
Shunned by greater society
Those who care are caretakers
Staff to show you "the ropes"
Written out of society
With untapped potential
"They can't be taught"
In reality, find the way they learn
New ways to teach
New ways to experience life
Everyone could be someone
You have a disability
Disability doesn't have you
Fight your way into the light
Make yourself seen
You are unlike-minded
You are warriors in your own fight

# Tis Her Season

Her air is cool and crisp
Though passions are hot
Her leaves fall
Making way for new growth
Bringing joy to those around her
The weather of bundling up
Cuddling and warmth
To truly know her
Is to love her deeply
A raging fire burns inside
Though she is calm and collected
Her passions run deep
Her love is true
This, now, her season too
Year round she burns true

## To top or Bottom

Disrobing slowly
Anticipation is killing us
Lips against lips
Feeling your thickness grow
Licking the lollipop
Throbbing and bouncing
Lusting and craving
Your warmth pressed against mine
Wanting to feel your thickness
Thrust within
Our thickness together
Deep in the heat of passion
Taking turns dominating
The deepness of our being
The feel of your cream
Within my passion
Hot and steamy
our forbiddeness grows
We are free together
Within the sheets
The release of inhibitions
Within each other
We lust for it all over again

# A Struggling Man

Alone in a dark room, you await
Unaware what you wait for
The distance brings a figure closer
Shrouded within the dark
Illuminated by his own light within
Slowly he approaches
Clutching possessions prized only by him
A newfound glory radiates from him
As if cured
Wicked wonders that plagued him
No longer eat him alive
With his typical smile he greets you
Why is he here?
Why now?
Assurance flows from him
"I will soon be ok"
A flood of sorrow flows from nowhere
Why are you telling me this?
You can't go, not now!
In the darkness he fades
Leaving you alone, in the dark
As if electrified you wake
Knowing in reality he still struggles
Because he knows not, who he is anymore

Who you are
Where he is
Trapped inside his mind
A most horrific prison
Now you wonder
When will he be set free?

# Welcoming an End

So much in my head
Intrusive thoughts
Sadness all around
So much loss to deal with
No one really cares
Keeping it all to myself
Suffering in silence
Dark thoughts invade
A voice encouraging me
End the pain
Find the shine
Drag it deep
Grab a woven
Dangle quietly
Overuse the tiny
Won't wake tomorrow
Encouraging a welcomed end
An end to the suffering
End of existence
Who really cares anyway
Just write the last letter
Say your goodbyes
It's over

# Little Angel

Remembering your tiny hand
Gripping as tight as you could
As if to tell me you will be ok
Such a short time to know you
Short time to hold you
Little diapers
Huge amounts of love
Those tiny blue eyes
Remembering you gripping the stuffy
Never letting it go
Until that day
You let us all go
The day you got your wings
The day you got your new job
Looking over us all
Checking in on us all
I missed out on so much
Missed first words
Lost first steps
Walking you in your white dress
All gone
Now you're my little angel
But always my lovely little lady

# My Dearest Lady

It's hard to not think of you
You swim in my head
A mystical woman
I never knew of
It's hard not experiencing your scent
That sweet smell radiating from your every being
It's difficult not tasting you on my lips
The taste of your sweet lips
I want to hold you for all time
Never letting you go
The sun shines brightly
The moment you enter the room
My woes melt away
The moment you say hello
It's difficult to breath
Without you by my side
A connection like no other
As if to span across multiple lives
A love so deep
Yet so bright
My dearest lady

I am now complete

# I Lay Aside My Sleeping Wife

Staring about the dimly lit room…
Warped shadows aloft above
Resume the shape of the memories invading
I lay here, a look upon those figures I see…
That only I can manifest, from my own guilt as they haunt me
The cat revives my attention from them with a slight rub of the face and purr in the ear.
Cat knows they aren't there, but she doesn't judge…
She only reminds, that I argue with my own thoughts, not a materialized being, I think I see.
Thoughts race within the highways of the mind
Like thousands of drunk drivers let loose behind the wheel
A dangerous past time thinking can be, with all that I have within my mind
Yes, some thoughts are happy, but these days….
Negativity and remembering the awful becomes prevalent, causing a chain reaction that even effects the body.
Ridiculous thoughts about actions to end the suffering and "make others happy once again" invade unwanted, and start to make sense at times.

But it's two little men molded after 'us', and this wonderful woman that sleeps next to me, that silences those days, bringing me back around.

As I lay here wide awake, I wonder why these thoughts keep me this way so many nights.

How I do hate thoughts like these.

# Join Me

Deep in the darkness
The whispers are so loud
Deafening and small
Calling to me
A light shines deep in the dark
Familiar faces distort
Recognizable
Yet wrong
The gone are here
Long from this world
Loved by me
Loved by others
Whispering in the dark
Reminding you of the glint you hold
Tales of the rope are told
Begging you to play along
Loved ones long gone
Missing you so
Begging you to follow
Join us now
It's so easy
The pain will end
I promise
I wake
I cry
Because I'm not sure I want to die

# Cravings

Smoke signals sent
I lust
I crave
I need
Lips across lips
Across the warmth of your being
To feel the passion emanating from you
Disrobe you slowly
The warmth of skin
Smooth sheets pressed on our body
To feel the knows of lust grow
Licking them so slightly
Feeling your pulse
Through your button
Across my tongue
The feel of womanhood
Tightly wrapped in my lust
Shortened breath
With quickened thrust
The feel of your explosion
Alongside mine
The heat of passion between us
And a long-awaited collapse of inhibitions
I lust your being

I crave your love
I need to feel you with me
However long it takes

# Once in a While

Decide
Even if it's hard
The suffering of others is real
Just don't add to it
Step back
Walk
Sometimes that's how you help
Ripping you apart
But it's the right thing
Right?
Destroys you inside
Yet they need to heal
It's what you do when you care
The pain is immense
But you will heal too
Will it come back?
Maybe someday
Be supportive
Be a good man
Hope for the best
Once in a while
Great things come back to you

# Will I…

Sleepy time
Say goodnight?
Say goodbye?
Will I wake?
I don't know
Click click
It didn't work this time
Will I wake?
I did this time
Take the bottle, please
I have taken enough
Will I wake?
I did this time
Find the glint
Drag it down
Will I wake?
Who really cares?

# Deep in the Shine

Stare into it
Looking back on one's self
Staring into the soul
See your every intention
You hate what you see
Staring back at you
You hate the man you have become
The man they made you
The things you had to do
The horrors you have seen
Pep talks in the shine
Are now a thing of the past
Insane conversations
Replace that now
Talk yourself out of an end
This is your silence
This is your torture
You suffer alone now
Staring deep into the shine
You try to love what you see
Taking others advise
But you can't love what you see
Spending so much time with hatred
Shaking hands with loathing

You can't forgive yourself yet
You need to be punished first
Deep in the shine
You're afraid
Of yourself

# Open Yourself

Trial by fire
Just jerk the wheel
This watery grave of mine
Drag it across
Open it up
Let the pain flow
Sweet, sweet, steel
Swallowed whole
Tiny but mighty
All at once swallowed
Long walk meet short peer
So many ways I open up to you
I wait for you
The inevitable end
Escape only happens a few times
Eventually, we will meet
Open yourself, or be opened
One way or another, we will meet

# Black Hole

Surrounded by people
I'm still alone
Darkness eats
Hollow and yet full
The pain is all I know
Thoughts invade me
Intruders of the mind
The urge is real
End is always in sight
The black hole devours me
Takes control of me
Escape is no option
A few sparks fly
Deep in the darkness
Something to reach for
Someone to love
The sparks bring me round
The darkness ain't so dark now
Endings aren't so tempting
My sparks are real
They want to be here
Want me to be here
And maybe
Just maybe

I might want to be too
The black hole is shrinking
Thanks to my sparks in the darkness

# The Sadness of Children

Time to sit
It's time to tell
A saddened child breaks
His wife breaks with him
The sad story told
But the child's babies are strong
Stronger than him
Feelings get buried
The babies won't cry
Not yet, not now
The child's sadness and anger has boiled
Boiled within
Why must she go
A queen, the matriarch of old
Alone, she suffers
As the child is too far away
So together we wait
For the final day
Together we fight
The sadness of children

# Slow Believers

Time and time again in life
Our metal is tested
Life tests your willingness to live
Tempting the hidden longing to leave
Reset our lives anew
The evils that live within will do their best
Their best to make you give up your fight
The everyday fight to get out of bed
That everyday willingness to push past it all
Continuing to live each day
Living for yourself
Pushing past the evils that slow you down
Past those thoughts that haunt your mind
Seeing through the guilt-stained hands
To see your inner self
Feed the good thoughts
Let flourish the love in your heart
For even slow believers such as myself
Can see the hint of silver in that dark cloud
And hope for the sun to shine again

# Broken Friends

A broken man watches from afar
A broken friend pours sorrow onto a digital wall
The broken man worries from afar
As his broken friend falls apart
What could it be,
Who does this message on the wall talk to
Could he be awaiting an end?
The broken man hopes for a start for him
Praying it's not the end for a friend

The broken man dies inside and weeps
The broken friend lay broken in liquid rose
A broken man weeps his days away
As he hates and punishes a blind self
Blind to the friend's needs.
Deaf to the friend's call.
How did the broken man not see this coming?
Why didn't the broken friend get help
Ask the broken man,
For a timeless tax on the friendship
A one-time fee of a shoulder to cry on.
That tax of a good ear to talk to.

Moving on years later

The broken man lays on the bed breaking more
Anger has replaced the fun-loving man
Hatred replaces good man once there
A broken angel whispers to him…
"Don't fret my broken friend, for I am ok"
"Don't repeat my mistake, talk about what bothers you"
So again we sit in that chair, the broken friend
Putting the pieces of a broken life together.
Talk to your broken friends, don't make my mistake
I didn't catch my broken friend before he fell

# Rage Drunk

Thirst it
Desire it
Feel the power that fills you up
That drunk light-head you get
The anger builds and fills the pores of your soul
You thirst for the venom that pours into your mind
The poison that floods your veins,
Burns you from within
That sudden power you're consumed by
When rage and anger become you
This is my therapy
Here is the outlet of my soul
For I can be dangerous to myself
The power is a danger to others
Because I hold it all in,
I. Am. Rage drunk

\*\*This is more of an outlet for an issue that was angering me, but I used it as an opportunity to generalize it. Hoping to relate to others out there who suffer from anger issues, get help friend, because we can get through it\*\*

# New Beginnings

It begins with a proud woman.
Shrouded in robes of splendour
With a confident walk and head held high
She gestures in remembrance of the fallen father
Starting the beginning of a new life
 Life with a loving family she barely knew
A family exceedingly proud of the woman's accomplishments
 With loss of father, then abandoned by others
A drive like no other proved to Carry her on
Her insistence to "stick with it" impressed those close to her
 Her determination only rivaled by the best of humanity itself
An easy way out was not a viable option for her
She is loved and adored by those around her
Admired by her loving family
With her new beginnings, shall come success
 Her proven determination is her ally
With new beginnings shall bring a healing force sealing her past.
She is my little sister, my friend, my hero…
She has my admiration, my love, and protection
 As I would any family member with her

# Changes Irreversible?

Even the slightest of actions,
smallest of introductions…
 Will insight change in your world
 Even the hardest of men will change
Even the smallest of actions
 Good or bad
Can change the world around you.
Little by little picking apart our surroundings
 Peeling back the layer of social standings
 Driving through those we see, others don't
Forcing that plight of ignorance
 The coat falsely giving off confidence
All the while aquiver with deafening fright
Drenched in social stigma
This new animal, new person, new situation
Causes a slight rewire in the day
With the greatest of ease
I panic and tear apart the inner workings
 With a quickness I devour the air around me
Thickening what's left , stagnating the rest
Even the slightest change causes stress
Drives me mad beyond any norm…
Oh how change can devour a man
Insights madness

Frees the delightful darkness within
All while they laugh
No one sees them point at you
Only you see them mocking
Hear their horror
Please, Shut them up…

# Me

At my weakest point, I am strong
At my strongest point, things are fragile
At my heaviest point, I was waiting for death
At my lightest points, I seen miracles of birth
At my widest point, I stood out in the crowd
At my thinnest point, I was just a number
At my most normal point, I was a "green" child
At my most "seasoned" point, I am near crazy
At my liveliest point, I still hated life
Now as I begin to love life
I'm boring

# A Mental Hostage

No amount of meds rids you of the pain
Keep yourself busy and ignore the sounds
That nagging whisper
The silent argument
Played on loop
You see them, you hear them
Please, is it not true?
It's a falsity created in your mind
 That only you hear and see
This horror you must face alone
Your music pumping can't drown them out
With no certainty can your doctor rid you of them
So again the nagging whispers
The silent arguments
Haunt you through the day
Peeling back your will to go on
Little by little you want to give up
Each night you cry out to them
"Why do you haunt me so?"
Giving in to your withering criticism
 You see yourself as a monster
Because "they" say you are

# Within the Fires of Rage

In the darkened corners of the soul
Hidden deep away from all
Hoping it never happens to surface
The broiling fire burns within
For decades I feed it
Tending the fire that comforted me so
Even the smallest thing breaths life to it
Turning to the fire when I feel alone
Over time the fire is not only part of me
It consumes me, creates a bitter man
Fuelled from a hated child
Made anew with a handsy uncle
He began the process that created this
Fuelling and breathing life to the rage
A broken and scared shell of a boy
Became a rage consumed man before you
Growing to hate the world,
Now I am lost in an attempt to extinguish
Before I am no longer…
Before I become nothing more
A permanent fixture within the fires of rage

# A Tale of Self Hate

The struggle continued each and everyday
A hatred for the one who looks upon me
The creature that stares back from the glare
The slob that greets my presence
I see them there, a mocking smile
You will never be better than me
Never amount to your potential
Love will always escape you
You will never see those who care
You look familiar to me
But I do not know this person
The one who stares back at me
Winking, waving, copying me
But as I look through the mirror
The creature I see is not to be
They are not who I wish to be me
I see myself much different inside
I wish to be thinner
Maybe more muscular
Not this slob I see
But why can't the me they see
All of them see a more deserving
More desirable me

So why can't I see that me
Why do I see this me
So it continued
This silent tale of self hate
Why do I hate me?

# Direction is a Loss

West of sanity is our minds
Not quite reaching the pinnacle of complete loss
Just within the boundaries
Yet far beyond the reaches of hope
Deep in the shadows of the mind
Ripping and eating the soul
This insanity and hurt create our hive
A hive mind pulling us to our common centre
The VA, our Umbrella corporation
Pulling the already taut strings of our mind
In hopes of hearing the music of sorrow
The all too familiar twang of the tortured heart
Thousands of remixes, and covers
All of the same hurt, all the same song
Many different versions, of that same song
We pour our heart out, in hopes of a magic fix
But they only hear the blah blah blah
Hardly any care, and most just wanna medicate
Our tortured mind, body, and soul…
Is not your lab rats,
Where are the caring few
Those few who will pull you from the dark
Show you the light around you
Too many of us no longer wanna feel

Too many give up that fight, to end that pain
Direction of the mind
Lost to the rest of me

# Good Night
## *written through the eyes of others*

Its finally that time
Time to say good night
To let it all be free
Free of worry
Pain
And doubt
More than anything
I want it to be over
This falsehood led everyday
To cater to you, nothing for me
It's time to say good night
Good night to a cruel world
A world that has no care
One that beats you when you're down
A world you can prove your right to…
…but still be wrong in the end
So good night world
I bid you farewell again
This time will be different though
As there will be no morning for this lonely traveller on your corrupt roads…
Good night

# Weaknesses of Cold Steel

A hardened outside
Complex and final
So many ways to hide the truth
Yet deep down inside, you're dying
Pockets of self hate
Whirlwinds of fear
You use humor to hide
Laughing but not happy
Wishing you were something you're not
And hating what you have become
Loathing decisions past
Disgusted with things you have done
But for all around you
You're a hardened human
Hardness of cold steel
Yet you're all mush inside
Wondering how you survive day to day
Convincing yourself you can't just run
You can't break
You can't end it all
That everyday battle within
To not show that weakened self
The one lurking just under the surface
Anxious to break through
Trying to break you
Will you fight?

# Uncle Hate

Put on a smile for the world to see... hide the pain deep and never allow it to seep through...
 For my pain is a torment that no human should endure. I can't ask anyone to share it with me ... only to push me through this poisoning cloud of self hate and doubt...
Help me through and love me while I fight...
For I will defeat this foe of mine one day...
I will meet you on the other side of hate and doubt....
To return the love you generously donated, provided to my pathetic cause...
Loving me can be a curse and torture, to see it first hand You must travel back to my own home, look upon those who tried and failed with me...
They have lost me in this cloud and cannot keep trying to find me...
So here I continue on this poisoning path of hate and distrust...
Six times I have fallen to my fate both of nature's way and most of my own choosing...
But an outside hope and light keeps me alive keeps me firm and strong enough to move on...
Your fumbling hands all over my childhood and perverted thoughts never kept me down...
I will beat this the way of the lost...
The way of the tormented...

# Find Me…

I am lost, withering away in the dark
Scared…
No … frightened
No … terrified
How did I get in here?
Where did I come in?
Where is the door?
I can hear them in here with me
Gnawing away at my peace
Drinking my sanity
Why did I come here?
Are answers this important?
Should have locked the door
Locking them away forever
Someone make them go away
I can't ignore them forever
Is anyone searching for the real me?
I'm locked away with them
Slowly they inch closer
Feeding on the fear
And the remainder of sanity
Their glowing eyes peer through me
As they witnessed it all in a flash
Growing stronger

Feeding on the pain
Someone come find me
…don' t leave me alone with them…

# A Broken Reflection

The man looks upon the reflective glass
Seeing a weathered and broken useless man
You can see the pain pouring from his eyes
His mental state deeply diminished
Deeply disturbed with visions of painful times
Invasions of bloody men, women, children
Thoughts of a war fought many years ago
Battles still waging in his head
Thoughts of self harm become prominent
The belief that he can no longer provide
Nor able to care for a family proper
Those become a staple of everyday life
Disturbing anger becomes a constant
Beloved tasks are just a burden
He hates himself and doesn't even want to be
Please take this all away
For he is tired
And wishes to be at peace

# Uncle Fumble Fingers

Can I unremember?
I still feel you looming over me
Staring down on me hungry
Eating my heart and trust one caress at a time
Feeling ugly
Feeling used…
So used … chewed bubble gum on my shoe used
I feel disgraced
Ripped in half


You were supposed to protect
Supposed to prevent
Not intend
Certainly not try me on for size
Destroyed my view of family
Nearly set my trust in all aflame
Wanting to curl up and forget … me
But I have remembered
I have found courage again…
Almost thirty years later
I fight you off me
I kick and scream
Tearing at your frightening image

I will fight out of my shadows
I will win this battle
I have been to war
Seen its destruction
Can I unremember you?
I don't need to anymore
You have made me stronger
Where I thought I was weak…
I will fight your storm of lust and anger
And through it all
I will row away in my life raft of hope…
And self worth…
Upon the waters of life
And I will tell the world about you
You're not my family anymore
You're the bad man who couldn't keep his hands to himself…
You won't touch me again

# The Torn

Ripped and shredded
I lay in waiting
Anxious for that moment
The point of no return
Around me the unseen…
But I see
Tormented and slaughtered
The everyday mind
Once a soldier, always a soldier
Buck up and drive on?
How?
Everyday a new challenge
Driving on, each day, because of family
Trying to shrug off that constant reminder
The unseen blame us
Blame me?
Everyday mind
Tormented
And torn

# Courage under his Abuses

She is here because of her joy
She is here due to her pain
She is here because of her act
She lives because of that strength
She is here because of her "fight"
She is imprisoned because "peers" said it was wrong
She is "free" because she had enough
She was imprisoned due to his rage
She was frightened everyday due to his acts
Everyday she feared for her life
She will heal over time
But forever be scared of a repeat offender in her mind
She bravely fought the pain
She dispatched his evil
She may be here with other offenders
Locked away for their acts
Shunned for their "rage"
But she smiles and faces the day anew
As she is now, free of his rage

# Greatness from struggle

Many years pass being held out afar
Arms out stretched
Like a woman disgusted with her child
The sight of me angered you so many years
So you kept me at bay
Struggling through life to feel true embrace
Never knowing if I was special
Or that constant reminder of him
Hate at every turn, rage at any door
Few guard my path but I am blind to their effort
Attempts to reach me, falling on an empty soul
I lived life to prove I am someone to you
In hopes to hear you're proud
Desperately seeking your approval
Struggling through the quicksand pit I cling to
Feverishly pushing myself to prove myself
Every step I lost who I am
Through war, and anguish I marched
All the while harbouring a deep disdain for the one I see reflected back to me
But each step brings me closer to greatness
This, I now see, the greatness in little faces
When they stare up at me in wonder
I am their superhero

They are my saviours
 I live my life for them, and my better half
For they are my legacy, my greatness
And I no longer live to impress you
Or seek approval for the man I have become
For the ones who approve, stare at me in wonder

# The Darkness of a Man

Alone in his head he hides away
Fighting for his life
Trying not to give in
A husband
A father
But in the darkness he is broken
Feeling useless
Hiding everything away
Can't let them see "me"
A false shroud for public
A broken man in private
His loved ones pick up the slack
While he hides and dies inside
Hiding in the dark
Doubting himself
Hating himself
Questioning his importance
Struggling against the call
Shielding others from his pain
Loved ones try to crack his egg
"Let it out" they say
But
Will his darkness make them run?
Or will he just give up?
Time to find that light
Time to take a chance

# My light Shining in the Dark

Alone in the darkness of my mind
I sit lost to myself
Horrors all around me
Defining silence and remorse
Slowly I see it
I see her
Shining the way
Like a candle that fights the wind
She beckons me out
Out from the dark
Saving me from the horror
Saving me from the suicidal jester
Saving me a little at a time
Returning everyday without fail
She is my light
That is shining in my dark

## Lost the Hero

Alone they fight
An unwinnable fight
Demons and thoughts
Win every time
Trying to fight for a life they lost
Lost this life when they left you behind
An unwanted life takes its place
They only know the emptiness
The hate
The anger
The depression that all builds within
Slowly, it takes over every fibre of them
Losing their true self
The loving person they used to be
The warmth in the heart is all
Loved ones are even unknown to them
Lost they feel alone
Only one thing to do
Only one out
Paint the walls
Decorated with a hero
The lost hero takes themselves away
Away from everyone
Tragic decoration
Hurry and save the lost hero

# Who Saves the "Hero"?

So now you're a "hero"
At least that's what THEY say
You did your job ... just a job
Under orders, you were someone else
Unspeakable horrors done
Unforgivable things were done
But they don't know
You fight for a country that sees you as a number
You "liberate" a country that doesn't want you there
In reality, you fight for hidden agendas
Nowadays, the view finder is clouded
Your mind is permanently set to horror
The suicidal jester bounces in your head
You have failed it in the past
So you joke and make light of it
But he still whispers to you to end it all
Those horrors are long over
But mentally, you're still there every day
You torture yourself in silence
Because who wants to listen to the "hero" cry
So what the hell makes you a "hero"?
You have been asking yourself that every day
But who saves the "hero" in crisis?


*das ist meine Geschichte*

# A Rush

Raging within
Wild and free
Cutting its own path
Nothing stands in its way
Free and clear of care
Carving its path
Unknown where it's gonna go
What obstacles it's gonna meet
It must touch you
Reach out for you
Feel you at night
It aches when you're not near
My heart
My love
I'm always here

# This Shell

Deep within this shell of mine
The dead parts of me flake away
Infesting and tainting it all
Dark and disturbed
Broken and bruised
Spreading like fire
Chasing away my truth
Distorting a fragile self
Burning away actuality
Now I'm infested
Twisted sense of worth
Withered away the love
A love for the one I see
Staring back through that looking glass
Hateful is the presence of mind
As I look on this shell of mine
I'm torn within
Infested with unwanted images
These thoughts infect my mind
Aching for actions I know mustn't happen
Crying out in silence for a saviour
Frightened of the darkened corners of the mind
Of the things lurking in the shadows
How do I save my truth

To save this withering and rotting shell
Anger and hatred consume me
Consuming this truth
Leaving a darkened broken shell

# Faithfully Abused, No longer Scared

Bound and determined
 I will take my life back from them…
A life dictated by my past
Influenced by the hate
Derailed by your abuse
You tried to ruin me
Tried to push me down
I may not know how yet…
But I'm gonna release that part of me
Send his broken and frail soul away.
This part of me is no longer needed
He is in the way, trying to ruin me
This part is your voice
The voice of hate, and unreasoning
I don't know when
Not sure how
But I will take back my life
From your systematical abuses
You cannot have me any more
You will not harm me any further

# Father Where Are You?

Where are you?
Are you that chill running over my back
Are you the whisper I hear behind me
Is that you I see in the corner of my eye
Maybe it's you I feel watching me sleep
Or the cold hand holding mine, as I weep
Maybe you're the voice, soothing me as I sleep
I hate that you were taken
Yet it feels as if you were never gone
I smell you always around me
I hear the boys, they chatter with you
I think I hear your voice, it guides me
As I lay here, in solitude, and damaged
I think I feel you there, trying to help
We, your family, weep in your absence
We grieve your untimely passing
The little ones say you're there…
I long to see you again, as well as she
She is hurt and damaged even more
In need of your guidance and love,
Where are you in this desperate time of need
It's those small reminders
Letting us know
You're still here
Good night, one more time
But where are you tonight … are you here

# You Can't Have Me!

I know you well
You have been a companion for years
You follow my every move
Creating barriers anywhere I go
Causing me to question myself
Question others around me
You have nearly become my entirety
Infiltrator of every thought
Raider of conscious minds
Looter of sanity
You pillage within the villages of my thoughts
Creating chaos at any turn
Breaking the concentration of even the most disciplined
Breaking the spirit of the brave, and trusted few
You rip us from our families
As some wish to suffer in silence,
Others cry out for a helping hand
Take my hand and we can conquer it together
Drag me away from these painful things
I know they are not real, but it's real enough
Some have given in to your ideals
Some felt sleep eternal was the only way
The way they can escape your grasp
You cannot have me

I will fight you every step
I will survive you
I'm not afraid of you, as I say your name
You will not win…
PTSD

# Societal Norms Be Abnormal

From the days as a child we trim them
Trimming away the abnormal, the "wrong"
Fit in the proverbial box, conform to our demands
Yes, creativity is allowed, but it must be approved
It must prove to fit our "laws"
Laws of humanity, rules of society
Your psychology must stay intact, don't stray
For straying from the "path" set before you,
Can prove to be a punishable offense
They will medicate you and set you right
For extreme cases, we are locked away
Forgotten and shunned from those who matter
You search for love within, and yet it's not found
Search outward, but conform to the norm…
As anything off track will upset that order craved
Dare to be different, answer the desires within, and your looked upon with hate and mistrust
I implore you, I beg you, upset the order
Be yourselves, be the you that you were born to be
Give in to your lusts and desires, love those around you
If being yourself means you desire the same sex, then so be it … It is you who needs to love
It is you that must remain "alive and fulfilled"
Enjoy yourself as you were meant to be
Because in the end
The social norm, is to be abnormal

# Bully!

How sad the bully made her
How sad it is seeing this tragedy
Watching her dangle and swing
Back and forth
Confined by the rope
How desperate she seems
Just swinging in the wind
How long could she hold on
All alone she swings at the end of it all
Warmth draining from her on this cold day
She torments me with her life
As she swings there watching me go
Watching me set myself free
How sad it is that of my depression
As she taunts me with her free will
They all love her
And show hate for me
It all WAS painful for a while
As I once cried myself to sleep
Bullied so much
Home, and in school
There was no break from it all
But, I have freed myself
Set my pain free

As I swing here and leave you all behind
I'm free now, no more bullies
No more yelling at home
No more, Mom's boyfriend and his wandering hands
You have your favourite child left
My clone, but still treated so different
Good night to you all
I bid you all farewell
I am free

# Living in a Haze

From the time of kinder
It's been a horror
Living there was a nightmare
Reminding you of your mistakes
Hated for your choice
Always second class
Never on that pedestal
The troll who lived beneath
The dishwasher who moved out
The maid who left
Frozen by your cold shoulder
All alone in my life
Walking in my haze
But I am loved now
Shown a real life
You can't stand it
So goodbye
Goodbye, tyrant

# The Darkness of Light

Alone in this dwelling
The mind races
Depression sets in
Unwanted thoughts set in
THEY are so prevalent
THEY cannot be ignored
So much could be done around here
Yet I'm paralyzed with fear and dread
The dwelling fades
As memory serves me injustice
Harmful thoughts dance in the head
"Do it" the voices say
Am I really this horrible person
The mind makes me believe so
Alone in the dark I sit
Punishing myself again

# You Don't Know

Alone in the dark of his mind
He contemplates a quick end
Styles and designs
And how to's
Feeling alone, he expires away
So many times he feels it's the only answer
But you don't know
You have talked him out of it
You might be small
You might be innocent
You have introduced new beauty into his life
You have brought a light into the dark
You have shown him love
Where no one ever bothered
Where others only show hate
You gave him strength
When he felt only weakness
So much effort to lift him up
When he is at his lowest
"Needing him" when he felt insignificant
Surprised him with love at every turn
When he was isolated in the dark
You all brought even the littlest bit of joy
When he thought there was none

Calmed him when he was furious
What you all don't know
You talk him out of it every day
Making him realize
It's gonna eventually be ok

www.ingramcontent.com/pod-product-compliance
Lightning Source LLC
LaVergne TN
LVHW041647060526
838200LV00040B/1744